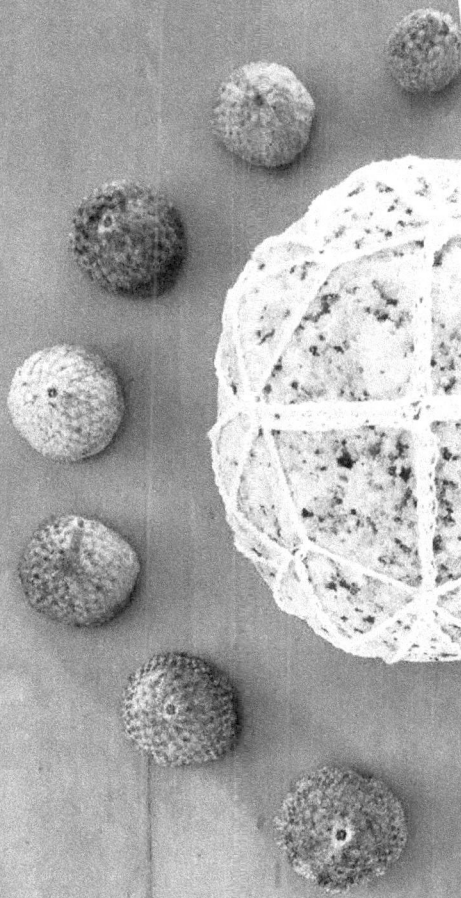
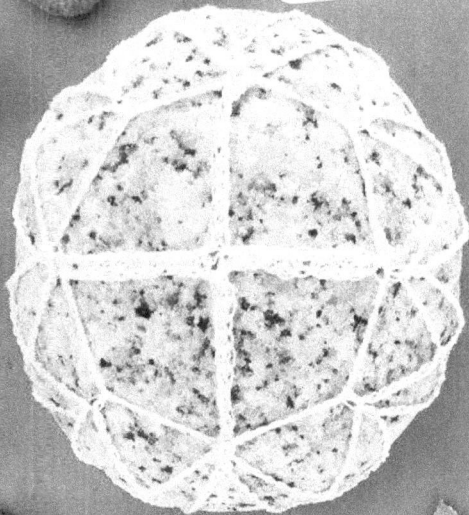

Conversations with Gravel

by Sarah Thursday

Copyright 2018 Sadie Girl Press
Cover and interior art
by Jennifer Takahashi
Cover and interior layout and design
by Sarah Thursday
Editing assistance by Terry Ann Wright
ISBN-13: 978-0-9978155-7-3

For all those made of stardust but living as gravel.

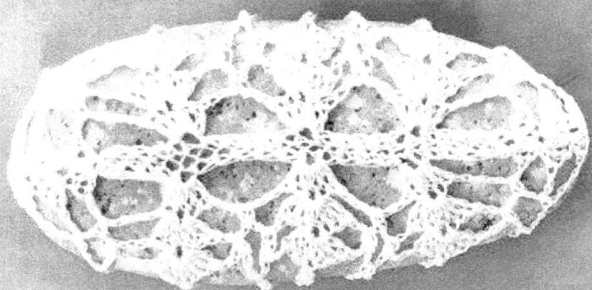

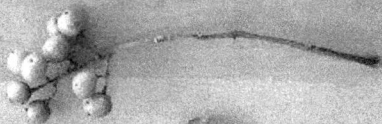

Contents

Acknowledgements   103

Gravel

you were once collapsing clouds of stardust
transformed into nebula
compressed into molten core of earth
you became magma
suddenly, spewed up to sky
you were lava
hardened into igneous
you became bedrock
after eternities, cracked from mountain
you were boulder
slowly, you were crushed under gravity
you became stone
broken again and again and again
you are gravel
over time, wind and water wear you away
you become stardust

Nebula to Magma

Palm Springs

I was in love at the desert's edge
inhaling the summer night
peeling a wet bathing suit
exhausting a hotel bed
like piñata candy
condom wrappers littered the floor
I found midnight stars
matched the freckles on your arms
somewhere between the pool
and shower and terrycloth robes
we found saturation
found forget
in a white-walled hotel room
under the desert sky

Unnamed Color

If I were a painter, I'd find the darkest
blue paint—thick as gravy—
push it slow across a powder-white
canvas, diagonal edge to edge,
let the ridges and valleys of the stroke
seep into a settled mass. I'd drag
the brush saturated in blue past
the easel, over my window pane
across my pale green wall
and onto my bed frame. I'd shape
the prints of my hands where I held
myself above you. Where I saw
you under me like a child, like one
who never married, never had children,
never worked twenty years in the same
company, never had to harden his heart
like police armor. I'd paint
the color of your eyes—
if they could ever be captured
in a shade made by man.

Cupcake

Your words,
frosting in my eyes.
Careful
as constant, how you
platter your smile.
I'm overdosed on sweet.
Crave the salt
of your neck. The melt
of your hands in my shoulders.
All the players are waving Vaseline
smiles behind shop windows.
They keep the lights on all night,
so really, I never sleep.
Outside you, I'm tired.
Want to smash windows
and grind glass
into porcelain mouths.
What if my love is only stone
for your now steady?
Will I ever be house,
cookie-baked warm after dinner?

Diamond

you gave me glimmer
in my hands
I called it *diamond*
for six weeks
I was wealthy
you called me *beauty*
you called me *art*
I was sultan
for six weeks
I held your jewel in my teeth
until it shattered
you called it *glass*
broken shards you swept
into piles in the trash

then you left me seed
in tiny green shells
for six weeks
I was fertile
you said *not over, not ready*
you said *maybe*
every dark morning
a new one dropped
onto my tongue
for six weeks
I waited for green
to break from black earth
until you called it *gravel*
kicked them like stones
across puddles
into the sewer

I tried to smooth the edges
tongue to teeth
teeth to tongue
for months
I held your pieces
tried to make you *mosaic*
turn the art of you
into mural across my chest
I dug up your empty shells
ground them into sand
crushed them
into diamond

Liquid Forget

I keep taking the wrong pills. The blue ones make the clouds grow thick. Heavy with doubt. The white makes the clouds angry electric. These tiny black pills bring icy air from open windows. (I can never find the right sweater.) The red ones, they make the tides under my chest heave and fall. They make the surface of my lips taste like longing. The pale yellow pills, if taken with the blue, burn his image on all four corners of my eyes. All refuse to look my way, all ache with beauty, all stare silent. The liquid green are meant to help me forget the hurricanes in my mind. But I forget what I forget and, forget what we promised and, I forget if I believe you and, I forget how your fingers felt laced between mine. Forget if we ever made love or just fucked or had sex or slept bare naked with your head on my shoulder. (Could I hear you breathing?) I take my pills. I still, remember too much.

The Case for Electricity

He was less electricity, more like down feathers
in a blanket to crawl under.
Except these feathers were still attached to wings
fixed on a bird in flight.
I clawed onto his back, smelled his fear and adrenaline,
his whiskey and love.
I fell deep for the sound of his voice
not the words of his mouth.
He was all downy-warmth and racing heart.
I forgot about electricity.

I lost my grip. I broke my wrists against the ground
feathers scattered, got caught in my throat.
I couldn't sing for months.
Every part of me ached for the frequency
tuned to the vibrations of his heart.
But I forgot about electricity.

We never discovered the currents of each other.
How two minds light up as they navigate
across their synapses
mapping stimuli in the expedition of souls.
These explorers will stay up talking for hours,
every watt, every jolt, every circuit path,
a new discovery.
We never stayed up talking for hours.

I fell, instead, for the downy of his voice
traded electricity for feathers.
Our flight would never have been sustained
by whiskey and adrenaline.

Girl in Flight

I envy the girls
with light-filled wings
They fly from breeze to breeze
pouring beams from their teeth
All men audience them
eat their smiles like candy
They breathe in love—
they breathe out love
No man ever
centers their universe

I could not be that girl for you
one with laughing eyelashes
smooth cheeks glossed
for kissing and leaving
kissing and leaving

I am unwinged, gravity locked
in oceans—not sky
teeth for crushing chains
eyes fire-fed
to burn through hurricanes

My love is anchor
my love is whale song
my love is sandpaper grit
galaxies inside pearl
volcanoes under mountain

My love does not breeze—
but tunnels into mantle
burrows into core
You want a girl in flight
laughing eyelashes
but I am unwinged gravity

Oceans Once Receded

I was a desert woman
who learned to live on cactus boys
learned to run at night and sleep all day
knowing the burn of sky and sand

Then you came with your oceans
rivers, lakes, and waterfalls
I dove in, eyes closed
hoping you'd teach me to swim
hoping to learn your whale songs

I threw away my land shoes
swam under the stars
let my skin pucker in your waves
my desert plants were drowning
I let them bloat and drift away

Then your tsunami receded
first sudden, then steady and slow
I stood naked in your mud bed
for weeks with dripping hair
dripping hands refused to dry

I learned to pray to wet earth
give thanks for saltwater baths
learned to hear your voice
in the night bird songs

Until even the mud left
took its soft clay from between my toes
the caked earth in my hair
began to dry and crumble
desert wind wiped all traces
of salt from my cheeks

I pulled myself back into desert shade
live now in the evening light
I can never return to cactus fruit
when I've fed on fields of phytoplankton
I've lost the taste for prickly boys
so I may wither for a while

Until at the edge of some moment
in the pale space between sun and moon
I might hear the sound
            of water rushing

Crescendo or What I Choose to Remember

The last time was unremarkable.
The last time with him was ordinary
in its duration, its position, its intensity.
That is to say, it was one more time before
he was off to work. One more time being
that it was the second time that morning.
The first time being everything the last
should have been. The first time that morning
was consumed starvation. Being that he made
my body forget gravity. The first time being laid
gasping off the side of the mattress.
It was the culmination of months abandoning.
The synchronicity of his chest against my shoulder
blades. The last time he set me altar high
and drowning in his sweat. The last time he'd fuck
anyone else on that mattress. He left me in love
with college boy sheets and summer fans
in November. The last time was a muted sigh.
The first time being crescendo. Arms tangled
in thighs. He refused to have me exhale
on his behalf. Being that he made my body
forget about gravity.

Passing Sounds Fade

The heavy of his arm around
my shoulders, the lack of weight—
how it sits there like a machine fitting,
clock-watch piece.
The dust in his voice lies
thick under my chest.
I know his closet is full
and the bodies are fresh
but I press against
the door with him. Spring
cleaning is months away. It's fall now,
so I rest my hands on his
warm coat, my hands against
his chest feel the *beat to breath*—
beat to breath. Close my eyes
and pray to an unknown god,
pray the planes will pass,
pray he isn't looking back.

Paper Airplane

We keep gnawing at roots
sopping in alcohol.
I am full. You still starve.

You want me bath-soaked,
I need you tree-hollow.
So I tear at your bark skin

until you bleed spoiled sugar.
Open my fingers and peel sunset
leaves from my palms.

Spit the pulp from my tongue,
lay it flat into perfect white rectangles,
press out every last drop of rain.

Let sunlight inhale what's left.
Even your teeth hate
how little I want to kiss you.

As you wither, I fold you in half,
crease your edges. Nose you forward.
Refuse to watch what happens next.

When I've said all the words I can say

I can only sound.
I dissonance.
I shutter volume.

I scrape metal to metal
–skyscraper groans
–car alarm until it backgrounds.

I tree crack from roots
–siren ambulance, fire truck.
I bone crush
–violin in a cold, dark alley.

I canyon scream
behind double pane windows.
You, inside, sit soundless.

How to Unexist

Go from friend to flirt to lover. Do it fast and without remorse. Stay lover for days or weeks until you become mistress. Be a good mistress until you become secret. Stay secret until you lose the key to his car. Then become lie, not a lie you've told but be a lie. Stay lie until your fingers break and you can no longer touch. Then become weight around a neck. One to be carried as heavy as regret. Stay weight until you become formality. Then, become cordial. Become a multiple-choice response of *hello, how are you, I'm fine, you're fine, we're fine, everyone is fine* until your fineness becomes echo. Stay echo while you begin to scrape your insides out. Pull out blood vessels. Pull out gut, fat, and muscle. Pull out bone. Lick it clean. Save your heart for last. Let it feel every ounce emptying. Then become translucent. Become as clear as ice so when he looks at you he sees nothing. Hears nothing. Feels nothing. Stay clear until you become forget. Become forget until all previous days dissolve. Stay forget until it never was. Until you are not even ghost. You are just not. Just no.

To myself in grief state

you don't believe you know how to grieve. death loss feels different from heartbreak, sits wrong in you. you keep moving your mouth from hour to hour, minute to minute. you fear if your mouth isn't full of sound the ache will surge up and slump off your tongue. you surround yourself with people and want desperately for them to see through you. both in the way you can be unseen and in the way they see below your skin. you don't want them to ask because you hate the effort of simple answers. equally you hate the weight of darkening a party of light-faced people with your honest answers. you are a paradox of love and emptiness. you want sleep like submerging oceans. there will never be enough sleep. you forget and want to be forgotten. want to remember before when you were the light.

Mouth of Fireflies

What God there was in me saw
the God there was in him,
and it was beautiful. -Amélie Frank

he speaks floating sparks of light
and lights a thousand eyes around him
he won't follow their leaving paths
throws them out and lets them land
like seeds he'll never see grow

I chase the fireflies of his mouth
the ones that miss their mark
I want to catch them in jars
drink them to kill my own night-growing
they sky-float beyond my reach
past the dim canopy of city light

I once drank him like a fountain
my wet lips glowed for days
my eyes shone too bright for sleeping
maybe I only dreamt him at my mouth
since the universe won't return him
it steals his beauty for dreamers
and says, light your own fire

first you must crack your ribs
break them into brittle shards
cut your palms in your own grasp

next you must rub the sticks
of your rib bones fast
do this all on the inside
then sing out to the dark unknowing

your sparks aren't made for eyes
your sparks are made to burn hunger
burn the ache in their bellies
throw them out like seeds
don't wait for them to grow

Burnt Toast

The moment the muse
you immortalized—
by recounting the beauty
of his soft tongue
and the flecks
of light in his eyes,
who created oceans
of chemical surges
in your synapses—
the moment he
becomes unwinged
and terrestrial,
he becomes
a sharpened collage
of limp words
and selfies,
of serrated tongues
and flaccid roses.
How mortal and bland
he now seems.
How crisply you see
the high fever
of anger and sex
and love and loss
crumble in your teeth,
grind all that now-space
like burnt toast in your molars,
wishing you'd scraped
off the blackness
before you swallowed.

View at 4 A.M.

You, a landscape sloping
down into soft valleys
where I trace your bare
terrain outlined in moonlight,
I rest on your dark side
how you speak clearest
in silence still as mountain tops
I, lying in your slant night,
an eager traveler pulling
at your dawn, sunrise us—
turn and move earth in me.

Good Friday Morning

You, cocked smile
and smirking eye
come down into my open
waiting like a teenaged sunbather
happy to risk the burn

You shadow me warm
with sentinel arms
my hands will not
rebel against you
both of us clinging
to this fragile ease

Tomorrow you return
to the gnawing thirst
lock me outside while
you fight those demons
eating at your skin

I return to the fullness
of poetry and fire-fed dreams
empty of your shadows
empty of skin-fueled
present tense

Lava to Bedrock

Moment You Should Have Caged

Now, you know you need it.
Have always needed it.
The way he looked at you across
the seat of your compact car.
You plunged into his rabbit hole eyes.
When he kissed you, his mouth
marked a song on your lips. He exhaled
victory as he pulled away.
You knew in that moment
a newborn truth,
how it can never go back.
Give birth a hundred times,
but his ache against your mouth
will never return.
You should have slammed
your car doors shut
and stole him from moving time.
Should never have drove him back
to his car. You should have turned
left, exited the lot with his face
still moonlight dim,
tore out on the highway
green lights flashing.

Shouting Hunger

You shout from the mountain tops
cry out for the universe to feed your empty soul.
I place at your feet the feast of me
prepared for hours, each cut of meat seared tender
each bowl overflowing, each glass
of wine made from grapes crushed
by each syllable of your name.

I climb jagged rocks to serve you stars
plucked from my eyes
and placed on your plate.
Still you cry starvation, cover my platters
with the cloth of your history.
Both our hands are shaking.
Both leave here empty.

If you ask me what I want,

I want you unraveled
I want you edge-frayed
I want you seam-busted
threads dragging
I want you broken glass
and rusted gears
tornado torn
tsunami choking
I want you black-eyed
swollen-lipped
nose-bloodied
I want you raw
I want you singed
I want you fat pulled
off the bone
I want you diary-read
secrets on billboards
I want you spit out
I want you dried-up
dead flowers hanging
I want you burnt forest
and dry savannah
I want you limb-splayed
arms tied
and hands nailed
I want you teeth-cracked
you feet-blistered
and back broken

I want you heart-dead
voice-cracked
lost-souled
I want you motherless
and child-lost
I want you loveless
and ugly
I want you cheap
and fucked

Mercy Killing

The moment you reached up,
touched her shoulder blade,
and she reached up,
touched your spine—
both lingered, three seconds, five,
—that moment Hope crawled
into the coffin of us.

With that—the fourth and final blow—
she spoke the nails onto the edges.
I handed her my hammer,
the one you refused to touch.
She handed me a mercy killing,
gave me finality. I pushed
what was left of us out to sea,
let the end of us float too far
to pull back.

I sighed out months of dying—
sighed a sobbing release,
pulled out the last threads of you
from my gut, and I
began to breathe.

How I Stopped Naming Lost Things

This is where I don't know what's next
this is where I get lost in the desert
forty years of circle wandering

This is where I try to fill the cracks
this is where I see how much I can fit
how many pages I can write
how many nights of alcohol
pushing limits where I thought I'd stop
the line I wouldn't cross

This is where I close my eyes and lay back
in the thick sea salt floating
underneath stars I can never count
This is where I stop
naming anyone *friend* or *lover*

There is where I keep stirring
the increasing mess of me
dissolve the powder
I am pudding-thick and ready to serve

This is where I am the forest fire and
the arsonist and the fireman
mask-wearing and sweating smoke

This is where the word *you*
is cut out in tiny rectangles
and collected in bags for confetti

where I forget what clocks I am watching
what timeline I had to follow
all the things called *age appropriate*

This is where I am done
and done and done knowing
that I ever knew

Love Letter No.1: To My Pit Bull Self

I love the teeth of your love
how you pit bull deep
into the flesh of loving
How you make shrines
in the empty spaces,
abandoned apartments
Shrines to former residents
of borrowed books and toiletries
envelopes full of photographs
and letters in pen
How you never fill
the same space with new
but keep building out
expand the frames and floors
How you know when to change the locks
and when to nail it shut

I love how you calculate
estimate the risk
How you trust
the unnamed algorithm
the intuitive push, flashing "Yes,
love this one, let that one in!"
How soft your wrought-iron grip
holds every name tight
each face, its own story
each moment, a glass in your pane
How you refuse to argue
about the wrong
or right way to love

I love how love-greedy you get
How you collect time
and stuff it in bags and boxes
shove it on shelves, in closets
covering walls, blocking doorways
in empty apartments
You guard-dog this house
an unapologetic hoarder
How you refuse to purge it
refuse to loosen your grip
Set shrines in windowsills
light blood candles
There is always room
for more

Pulp-Plastered

I've changed my mind
I want the blood bath
the tar-stained fingernails
the gut-black stairwell

I've grown too good at defending
It's too quiet and forgetting
I want to pull out eyelashes
lick the spiny hairs

I've already been smattered
pulp-plastered, rib-caged
I learned to breathe in smoke
find oxygen hung on particles

I want to sink my teeth in
crack the porcelain
kiss the blood from the edge
of his full dark mouth

Get Smart Gets Smarter

Most days the walls to my heart
are secret agent safe
layers upon layers of trap doors
flip-twist-gadget locks
fingerprint and eye retina reading
infrared laser protected
I am a fortress of strength
and got-my-shit-togetherness

But once in a while a thief
finds the control panel to my heart
flips the switch of my insatiable desire
turns the dial of my heavy longing
and there are parts of my body
of which I am no longer in control

He presses the button on my self-doubt
pulls the lever and the gates fling open
The right placed word can untie me
my strings tangle in his voice
The scent of his neck above his collarbone
can seep into my skin like poison
dissolve my steadfast resolution
of keeping-my-head-clear-mindedness

Nimble hands can break secret codes
my legs give in to inner leaping
all peripheral vision tunnels

and long fingers grazed soft
across top-secret regions
can erase hours of reasoning
rational thought processing
instantly delete all stored data
of why he is no good for me

Conversations We Never Had

I'm broken, you say
as you slide the drawer
of your intestines
back into your gut
I'm broken too, I say
as I clamp the windows
of my shoulders
down across my back

I don't know if I'll ever
be whole again, you say
as you twist the knobs
of your eyes
deeper into your skull
I don't know if I have
ever been whole, I say
as I snap the latches
of my thighs
farther into my pelvic bone

sit with me awhile, you say
as you push the doors
of your palms
open a little wider
lie with me awhile, I say
as I lift the ladder
of my spine
up a little higher

How to Go Backwards

Remove hands. Remove tongue. Remove legs.
  Leave heart. Leave eyes. Leave voice.
Remove say.
  Leave said.
Remove fuck. Remove kiss and dark car.
  Leave ache and story.
Remove naked.
  Leave cold.
Remove knowing.
  Leave knowing.
Remove lover and want.
  Leave honest and cordial.
Remove betray. Remove conflict. Remove open.
  Leave close. Leave accept.
Remove complicated. Remove layers. Remove hold.
  Leave alone. Leave alone. Leave alone.

Slow Skinning

Unlike car crash, our death was slow—peeled first nippled-breasts and what you once called the art of my body. Tendons carved from feet, keeping me put. Each muscle layered in fat stretched out all dance and joy. Yanked next nails from fingers, sliced entire tips down to knuckles, every part that ever knew any part of you. Hooked knives dug into ears, scraped out song, scraped out music. Same hooks dove down throat, twisted cords of my own speak, tangled in steel, snapped from neck. Sawed each hair from scalp, sawed lashes from lids, sawed between thighs where your hands once reached. Eyes pinned open, I watch you crawl out from under us, watch you wrap your arms around Night. I watch Night curl her blood lips. Can't hear singing, can't speak you down to me, can't reach can't touch can't fight can't walk the other way. This is how we die with nobody watching.

Somatic

I can't treat you like phobia
try to desensitize you out of my skin
so that my muscle fibers
won't gather together
at the soft crease of your eyes

      you are not a fear to face
   at the height of a bridge
open my eyes and gaze
   at the depth of you
     lean forward and
              release

 I cannot see you spider
   across my arm
      and deep breathe
    out the shiver
you raise in me

you are less like fear
more like heroin
a need I must starve
from myself
fast out the hunger
until the follicles
in my hair
have escaped
your scent

I will not apologize

for not being
soft-lipped
doe-eyed
for not laughing
at all your jokes
and if I put my hand
on your shoulder
it will not be an invitation
if my fingers linger
which they will not
you will not have the rights to me
to my round parts
to my fullness
against your bare bones
I will not apologize
for not being
giggle-light
batted-lashes
but more
teeth barred
and fist clenched
my gaze always at the door
on the clock
holding breaths
waiting
for you to learn
my name is not prey

Cells Apart

You're sure the bleeding's stopped
the swelling's gone down
chance of infection slight to none

cut off the tourniquet
expose raw skin to open air
no sudden moves

wait for it

cells will draw themselves together
with the tips of your fingers over and over
you will trace the line to remember

you are miracle.

If Poetry Is Parked Car

My heart is bottom-pink
and raw, not knowing
how many beats to give
beats to exhale

All words crowd into the soft
spaces, roof of my mouth
cutting inside cheeks
rolling off lips

All quiets are questions
my voice too loud
my hands too clumsy

How do I protect you
when I've just been born?
When my spit edges
in the corners of your drink?

I'm dumb, backseat fumbling
legs over knees
arms over shoulders

If my skin in moonlight
is softest, how do your hands
melt into my scars?

Elephant

We dance under the belly of the elephant
not the dance-floor dance, but the slow move
around the words we won't say
move in and out of her shadow
Her dark cast allows our mouths to press our breath
around it, around the letters lost in open windows
I want you to press me full against elephant legs until
deep grooves of skin catch light
Her skin is your skin and the skin of your children
heavy with memory, pachyderm heavy
She shifts her weight and I wait for you to name her
call her out of decades, twenty-two years
You push off one finger to the other hand but
there it is in simple gold elephant eyes
Will you step out from under her
I cannot lean crouched here
swaying to your resonate voice
to the arch of your teeth
to the groove of your sleeve soft
underneath my fingertips
sliding down corduroy red

Unanswered

I see how he ruins his own beauty
how before he can leave for the bar
he follows can after can
to cool the fevers in his mind
how he leaves out food
for the fullness of cheap beer
thinks it makes him a tragic man
worthy of writing an elegy
he curses his drunken mother
between swigs from cold aluminum
asks about my birthday
he wants me to teach him
about how to clean the shower stall
I am nobody's mother
though I want to say
it begins with the need to be clean
but he asks again about my birthday
repeats back my answers
like he's committing it to memory
I refuse to be his fixer
only drag my nail-bitten fingers
through his unwashed hair
his mouth disappearing at my breast

What to Do with Empty Hands

I don't know what to do with my hands
I opened them up, I released my grip
the rope was ripped away
last strands tangled in my fingertips
so I cut one thread at a time
with the razor of my teeth

I still don't know what to do with my hands
I washed off the blood, cleaned out the burn
they are bandaged and gauzed
but my fingers keep curling
around the ghost of your wrists
I press them out flat against the shower wall
against my bedroom wall, one hand
against the other, finger to finger

I still don't know what to do with my hands
I've been writing you out of my heart for months
I run out of lead, I run out of paper
still my hands move around the ghost of your neck
your voice murmuring in the center of my palms
I try but I can't suffocate your shadows

I don't know what to do with my hands
so I press them to my mouth
let my lips surrender to your memory
I drag them everywhere you've been
across the back of my thighs
down the tip of my nose
they circle the round of my shoulder
(the last place you ever kissed me)

Boulder to Stone

Your Dark Sunlight

You, carried by wind, fill my horizon
I am tangled in your kite strings
knees bloody from the drag
arms ache from wind yanking

I squeeze eyelids tight
can't find sleep in your sunlight
eyes grow dark
circled by your high maybes

Your wild flight, soar and dive
I have no wings to carry
can't pull to your height
you only rise, grow farther

Hand me your knife
cut me clean of you
Let my wrists bleed and clot
let me fall asleep

in the quiet dark

Dead Song

I wait no more for your polite
I run no longer to your cordial
I let no wind carry
let no night star
I fight not for your uncertain
for your wander, for your lost
not for your stroke, not your soothe
No more gray ink
photograph gaze
No collar bone
valley of skin
I set fire to your words
I drown your colors
all swirl of rainbow
I lie in your grave of kindness
I cough out your breath
I spit you out
wipe the taste of you
from my mouth

Love Letter No. 5: To My Unsteady Breath

you start as the air between bodies
never knowing if you'll be drawn breath or exhale
but you are always in motion
until the stretch between bodies begins
and you become stir and twist
decent

without heat to keep you in suspension
you live in moments
on the edge of his steps away
withdrawal of warmth makes you heavy
you descend
in full sight of him

as he pulls on his winter coat
and worn leather boots
you settle in the dark space
under the stove
where you grime into grout

there are no swells here
just swirl and drift
you gather with the all the forgotten things
where light is always inches away
heat here is compression
all unwanted molecules melt into stuck
you can surrender
become that fire grit

or you can scream out to the universe
for a mass upheaval
for a deep cleansing behind the cracks
it may still be heavy
or might be gray swish and bubbled swirl
but it's motion again

swept out from under
you won't know direction
down a drain, into a sewer
as long as it's moving
you'll eventually meet ocean
and it will terrify you
how unimportant you'll be

but you'll catch current
swift and sure
maybe you'll crash
against a rock or a boat
be thrown upward

maybe then you'll become spray
maybe sunlight will catch you
warm cold cells enough to rise
light enough to join clouds

Last Thread

It's the last thread
that's so hard to cut

The chain's long broken
the rope's been unraveled

I've swum against the currents
I've surfaced near the shore

The thin line's still tangled
through ocean tide hair

It pulls out slow and shining
like a timeline of a story

So I tie it in a bow
around my finger tight

to remember
where I've been

Reef of Clouds

I am a car underwater
driving through seaweed and coral
you are shark swimming
circling, circling
I have forgotten how to breathe
so I pull on blue-grey sunbeams
escalating me upwards
my lungs eat dust particles
I am phytoplankton
as small as molecules
as massive as continents
sending breath into clouds
into horizons
you are pollution
black slug of fossil fuel
I will sleep in the crook
of your arms
make you drink
in my low tide
turn you starlight

Comfort of Cars at Night

Street lights pass *one-two-three-four*
light-dark, light-dark, *one-two-three*
white dim passing car windows *three-four*
left hand on the steering wheel *two-three*
right hand in mine *one-two* your night-lit face
glows, flickers *two-three-four* dark calm
in your eyes caught tree shadows reaching
one-two across your face *three-four*
for days *two-three* I kissed you in the dark
one-two you turn the wheel slow *three-four*
my hips press towards you *one-two*
left arm against your right, you squeeze
two-three tighter between my fingers
three-four I see beauty in your shadows
one-two you whisper, "I'm lost" *two-three*
you slow brake *one-two-three* draw S.O.S.
on dirty glass *three-four* my feet press
against the floor *two-three* I whisper back
two-three-four I'm here *one-two* right here

Monkey Bars & Golden Spokes

Let's go back
to when you hung
on my words like monkey bars
when you sighed the first time
you ever kissed me,
gave me lottery-winning eyes
when you kissed me again

Go back before
my words hung
like bars around your cell
before you clenched
your teeth
at the sound
of my need

Go back when
you studied the curves
of my mouth
sent me to work
each morning
with a tongue
full of blessing

Go back before
every word
had to be measured
and weighed

before an honest response
could mean
I may never again see
the golden spokes
of your irises

Back to when
we were both
eager passengers
Back before
our feet were heavy
with hesitation

Back when
we knew nothing
Back before
we could not forget

Circles for Words

Us and *Our*
became *That*
and what *happEND*
no *You* and *I*
but *It* and *Was*
boxed up
shelved
with photos
*un*taken
said again—
it's *un*personal
some*thing*
so intimate
made demon-
strative pronoun
can't be spoken
in *Now*-space
disrupts fragile
lines to keep
in, keep *out*
I never told no one
no*thing*, no person
doesn't know that
We ever were any
thing

What I Mean When I Say *Run*

Get out, get out
and into the world
a woman like me
would tie your hands with ropes
and hang them from her hips

Get out while you can
and let the wind carry you
a woman like me
would climb from under your boots
and into your pockets
lay you down heavy on her bed
just to rise above you

Get out and wander
be a wild bird
a woman like me
would clip your song feathers
and stuff them in her mouth
just to have your voice
seeping from her ears

Get out and make no promises
don't even say you won't
a woman like me
hangs on open window sills
burns her eyes on the driveway's end
holds all your words
like collected seashells
in her cupped hands

Get out and go far
take no existing path
a woman like me
would strip you naked
press you inside of her
memorize the turn in your face
in the dim light
she'd reach in and pull
all the strength you have left

Get out
She'll want to cut rings
from the center of your eyes
and string them like beads
around her neck

Get out
She'll envy the breath in your lungs

Get out
She'll put a straw to your mouth

Get out
She'll want you empty

Get out
She'll drain you cold as death
just so she can pour her blood
into your veins

Love Letter No. 3: To My Mending Self

You may begin to miss the grieving
the adrenaline heart thrashing in your ribcage
the coughing lungs asking permission to breathe
You may begin to hear all the quiets
humid silence scratching
each day confirming
this is it
this is all it will ever be

You may begin to miss the panic of hope
tangled in his kite strings
miss the fight, the battle, the bruise
miss kissing blood from rope-burned hands
You may begin to sleep through the night
to lack rebuttal
to forget to answer back

You may begin notice
the crevices in your wrists
the uneven scurry
of a black beetle across concrete
notice the sound of lead scraping paper
how it curls to the rub of an eraser
disappears like it was never there
to begin with

Keansburg Park, 2012

After a hurricane, you must sift through the rubble. Be it car or house or theme park ride, all loss is for grieving. For months you will bloody and purple searching for what's worth saving. On the news, there is always a small child who's managed to hide between the gaps. Keep searching for her. Or, if you're the one buried, make yourself heard. At some point they will begin to haul away the wreckage. They will want to clear land for rebuilding. But if you're still searching, be louder. Keep kicking through splintered wood and twisted metal. You cannot and will not find every savable piece but remember that small child. She could be under the Ferris wheel. At some point, you will also call off the search. You will also want to clear land. But be prepared. When you stand on the edge of the sifted soil, a new loss will settle in. As heavy as roller coaster. If you stare into the ache of what was never found, the weight may collapse you. The name of that child may trouble your sleep. You must find her. Use the old wood or the old metal but build a new park to welcome her home.

Damsel

I will never be damsel enough
to be claimed victory by savior
the way he swoops down
in her destroyed
sword out and crowned
I am without tower
without step-mother plotting
I need lover like home
not savior
not prince
I need lover like foundation
under bare feet

Before I Lie

Did you hear my words
before I spoke them?
Did you read my mind
before I thought it through?
The truth I tried to lie
in your arms. The reality
I hoped you would pretend
with me a little while.
Long enough to warm
my vacant chest,
enough to rise up this low tide
pull up from under and thrust
out to the highest edges of my skin
with a crashing swell so full
I'd sleep for days
without want
or need
of anything.

Weight of Light

I slept for days
like the end of a deep sigh
my head sunk tired, settled like dust
eyes too heavy for the weight of light
the manic song in my heart slowed down
for three whole days
my skin full of gratitude
opened itself to the night
and I laid at your side
covered in your dead scales
we let the revelers sing through morning
we let them stay awake for weeks
my heart sang *I am sleeping*
I am sleeping

Sediment

I've been sifting you for weeks
but there is no gold in your sediment
pebbles smooth against my tongue
I bed in your silver-grey sand
sleep in the warmth of your current
I keep losing daylight hours
forget my quest for real worth
I need to get up, get feet forward
find the strike to wealth me solid
foolish river, with your glittering light
I won't find gold in your sediment

How Quiet Kills

I speak you to the wind
and she carries the notes
of your name to the sky
I stand, hands empty
waiting for god
to speak you
back into my chest
but there is only
white
noise
blurred whispers
of everything
layer upon layer
of sound traffic
I speak again but find
no voice, no music
just cold
hands
open

Swore

As long as God
gives me breath,
you said.
As long as

God—you said.
Breath, you said.
You said—you said
—As long as

God gives
me—*as long*
as breath—you said.
God, you said.

Gives me, you said.
Long—*breath*—*God*—
me—you said. *Me,* you said.
You said, *As long as*

God gives me
breath, you said—
but God,
you still breathe.

Frost

When do we lay these sticks down?
Having been rubbed raw of revival
no sparks enough for flames—
I am too tired to promise I'll wait
faithful for another dawn.
You are more in love with saving the fire
than actually keeping us
warm and free from that frost that hangs
on branches above our heads—
it's been itching at us for years.
I'm going inside the house now,
I will leave the door unlocked
but I won't leave it open.
I won't call out to you again.
My words caught in cold breath
as I pull off wet feet,
hang them on wires
stretching for decades.
Say goodbye in white crystal
particles drifting into the black.

Gravel to Stardust

Fragile Beast

I made a promise to myself
to never again be the girl
who fell face flat for the ones
who must be pried open
constant banging on the door
let me in, prove
my hands are weaponless
all you fragile beasts
I'm not fighting
for you anymore
I resolve to remain here
at my station, not planted
at your door apologizing
for holding my breath
while you again
submerge

Where He Will Not Be

You know it.
You know he won't be there.
He won't be in the room
you are going into.
He will not be at his desk
or in the kitchen by the fridge.
You know this.
You say this to yourself
again and again.
It's just not possible.
You know this walking up the stairs.
You know this riding in the elevator.
You know this opening the door.
But five feet in— or even maybe ten,
you realize you've been holding your breath.
You hear footsteps.
It's not him.
You know this, of course.
You know.
But the disappointment pulls
the air from your lungs.
You need to inhale.
You need to exhale.
You need to do this
again and
again.

Scent Stained

You are the mistake I want to make
I will wrap myself in your red flags
and let you peel them off
one silk layer at a time

You are the regret I want to have
I'll bind you in my caution tape
lay on a bed of warning signs
cold metal against warm skin
cools your burning in my eyes

You are the fucked-up mess
I want to roll around in
like a mud-happy dog
drenched in your scent
I will not shake you out

How do you unsense me?

What I Mean When I Say *Ageless*

When we met for the first time—
not as friends—the first time as possibility,
you were aging in reverse past twenty years,
some fresh-faced boy fumbling for admiration.
You brushed my arm. Shoulders press and retreat.
I secretly hoped we'd never find our way home.

But your father face returned—I met this man
many months before. We were friends
but so much older. Eyes heavy with marriage
and house and family and work responsibility.

When we met again for the first time—
past possibility, in the space of immediate now
where time is irrelevant and skin speaks
all our words, your face became child.
When I counted the spokes in your irises,
I looked down at the escaping years
dissolving through your teeth.

Let's be children in some night parking lot
without the weight of older lives.
We'll climb into ours beds as all time—
as delinquency—as heavy sage—
as eager limbs—as singing rosies round
and round, spinning into the music.

Poem Without the Whole Truth About Sex

we never had great sex
we had not-exactly-an-affair sex
hurry-up-and-get-home-to-my-kids sex
we never had mind-blown sex
write-home-to-mother sex
we had stop-between-errands sex
forget-my-life-for-five-minutes sex
we had won't-look-you-in-the-eyes sex
don't-wrinkle-my-clothes sex
we never had first-waking-breath sex
never in-the-shower, -car, -kitchen, or -window sex
we had futon sex
we never had I'm-lucky-to-be-lying-next-to-you sex
never hot-make-up sex
we had let-me-call-you-"bad girl"-so-I-can-feel-less-bad
-about-just-needing-you-to-not-be-her sex
we never had I-love-you sex
never you-are-my-world sex
just had exploring-my-options sex
just if-I-keep-reminding-you-how-lost-I-am,
-you-won't-blame-me sex
never oh-my-fucking-god
can't-speak-after
where-did-that-come-from sex
just I-don't-know-who-I-am sex
just gotta-go sex
just sex

To the Men Who Told Me
My Love Was Not Enough

1. They told me with their hands

the first man I loved used his hands to pull down
my panties without asking
I had loved him without question
his carpenter hands
rough against my abdomen
my five-year-old heart was
blackhole becoming

2. They told me with their mouths

the second man I loved used his mouth
—when I gave him my free forward,
my unrelenting, my wide-open
when his empty was filled
with the red vacuum of my sex
he mouthed "I still love her"
and the *her* of me was vacated

3. They told me with their silence

the third man I loved used his tornadoed
soul against my earth-bed body for landing
then he pulled his sleeve up to his wrist
and wiped my name from his eyes,
rubbed my wetness from his now-landed
—took his relit fire and left
my heart, soot-thin
and never

Knife Wound

Did you choose me well?
Equal to her blade,
to match the knife
pulled out from your chest?
Or did you choose me as a sharper edge,
one to push much deeper?
Did you know how I'd cut,
how I'd slice clean into her skin?
  Am I the knife,
    or am I the gut?
      Why, now, are all of us bleeding?
        When you pull me out
      and she drains from you,
    will you put me back to whole?
  Or was I only ever your weapon?

Death by Rust

rust was the death of us
oxygen and iron
weather and time

hundreds of holes
have been patched
and painted over

restorations aren't made
of well-meanings
but of follow-throughs
and time-committed

we were not
the timeless classic
we set out to be

admit it
we've both been driving
other cars for years

our weakened frame became
overgrown by weeds
and nesting birds
while rust spread
under the belly of us

Tree Cutting

When pruning the branches of your soul
don't be afraid to cut deep.
It may leave scars but—
it will allow for more view of the sky.
The growth that follows
will flourish thicker, fuller.
But don't throw dead branches
into the street.
Let them lie at your roots,
decompose into basic elements—
hydrogen, oxygen, carbon,
sulfur, nitrogen, phosphorus.
Using water as a vessel, let the sun
pull the elements up through your limbs
and into the green of you.

Love Letter No. 4: To the Nail Biter

You will remember again
lying on a dry sunny beach
warm skin against rested bones.
This swim is not endless—
these swells you fight,
this constant coughing up water
will eventually subside.
Even the bleeding
edges of your cuticles
deserve your tenderness.
Because his hands will never
work that soothing magic again,
you must hold them away
from the sharpness of your teeth,
purse your lips,
and tell them they are as worthy
of your protection as your breasts,
as your pit-bull heart. As all of you
is worthy, so is the clear line
of your fingernails curving.
Cut them clean.
Even you, Olympic-storm swimmer,
can drag yourself up
on some long shore, wash the salt
from your skin, hold your hands up
to the sun and say it.
Say even your cuticles are worthy
of being loved.

What I Mean When I Say
We Can Talk Without Poetry

When I dance for you and our knees brush at the bar,
we begin to forget. The more I think about the space
inside your coat, the more you learn the names of my
favorite drinks, we stop   saying them. Words like
wife. Words like *marriage*. We become teenage-
nervous where mouths cannot form words like
separation. All I know is *giggle* and *heart-dotted-i's*. We
are back at the edge of unknowing. Where our
grownup selves are strangers we might not want to
meet. You use the word *awkward* when I give you a
book on a poet's *divorce*. You are a teenaged father all
over again. Except your children are leaving now, one
by one. You regress a decade for each one. If I am
fifteen and you are seventeen, sitting in my living room
listening to records, maybe we also forget the word
husband. You are just a boy with grown man scars. I am
only a girl biting my nails, chewing at the cuticles,
wishing that boy would lean down   and kiss me,
but fearing. Fearing if he does, it means we need more
words for *you* and *me*. And if you hold my hand, are we
steady? If I wear your coat wrapped around me in the
dark, what will be a word for that?

Pavlov's Lizard

Am I Pavlotic dog
lapping happy at flashing
green lights? Am I the bell
or the ring, trembling
at your sound?
Are there mountains rising
beyond these stars?
How many days until I lose
the taste of you? How many
hours until I wake? Am I
Twilight-Zoned into stupid
grins and daisy eyes?
If you are lizard, regrowing
limbs, can I collect severed arms
to quilt into a blanket
of your hands?

Funeral for Bees

I walk into swarming bees
to taste your honey. I
swallow sweet and sting
and comb alike. The hum
of your buzz and buzz
of your hum sticks golden
in my chest. The queen is
dying. You scratch and
mourn and bury her still
alive. Watch her wings
crush from collapsing
earth. You sing her floral
song with your failing
hands. I follow your
procession. Sway with
the bee-death dance. It's
the corners of your eyes I
want to kiss now. Lick
every last drop.

Eulogy

You keep having funerals
every day a new death
you have funerals for photographs
for cobwebs and empty spaces

You have a funeral for 20 years
every loss a ceremony
nothing formal, no eulogy
just your mourning eyes and silence

Every night the shoveling
every day the digging pit
no caskets or headstones
just a potter's field of memories

I'm choking on your dust
waiting for you to bury me
like old letters and anniversaries
like the women from your pen
washed in blue ink and smeared edges

You pour them like ash
into another grave
I've lost count of the hours
I tried to sway with your procession

I am waiting for soil to soak up sweat
soak up blood from failing veins
cover me in six feet of sky

It's me that needs to shovel earth
bury your corduroy and cover songs
bury late night texts and portraits in pen
bury keen eyes and melting hands
photographs we never took
memories we never made

When broken girls go to weddings—

when broken girls
with daddy issues
go to weddings
and see ex-lovers
taking selfies
with young girls—

when broken girls
with daddy issues
go to weddings
and watch ex-lovers'
hands rub against
the small of a woman's back—

when broken girls
see ex-lovers at a wedding
dancing with girls
half his age—
broken girls don't
catch bouquets

broken girls
with daddy issues
see a lover who saw
no worth in loving them—

broken girls
at weddings
drink more wine
than they mean to—

broken girls
with daddy issues
hate the men they love—
hate soft-voice men
who were supposed
to be better than
their fathers—

broken girls
with daddy issues
hate their bodies
when ex-lovers slide
their hands
around the waist
of a skinny girl—

broken girls
are done making friends
with pretty young girls
ex-lovers touch
while smiling

Record Scratch

How many times do we
replay the broken record
How many times do we
get up and jump the needle

Do we hold on for nostalgia's sake
Do those crackle-rich and cotton-
thick grooves sing better songs

How many repeats and repeats
until it's time to retire or never
Just resign ourselves to unrest
get up again and again

Records don't learn new songs
They don't unscratch or smooth out
We pack them up and
store them in our memories

Move on to modern times
where everything and everyone
is easily replaceable

Black, the Consumption of Song

It's still the music—
how it replaces the pulse in your veins
how it stops all the other voices,
your own cutthroat deafening.
You still swallow volume
guzzle it down like hard cider.
In that way, songs can sing from the inside out.
They balloon inside your heart
pressing up against limping muscle
until its ache rests in them.
You will always have it—
when love after love after love leaves
it still gets darker. Still you
wrap your skin in minor chords
mummy-tight until you can only move
in the way the rhythm sways.
You don't fight that.
For a while you are carried by it.
You rest in black—
how it still comforts you.
Sometimes and eventually music moves you
forward.
Slow beats for slow steps
when you are ready to hit the ground
on your own swollen feet.
For the rest of your days, you will—
as you always have—exhale melody.

Unknown Employee

I saw a girl at Target, she was me
at twenty-one years old.
She had my blond hair

and simple black-lined eyes,
a red vest and black band shirt
from Joy Division's *Unknown*

Pleasures. Iconic jagged white
mountain lines I once
plastered to my purse.

The image is a badge, I know
immediately, she is cool
in the way I was cool

working at Target at twenty-one.
I want to tell her we got bigger
plans, even if you can't see it now,

and that boy, who torments your soul,
is just passing by. I want to tell her
we end up alright, and all that confusion

might not get clear,
but it settles. And all that sadness,
the endless sadness fades away,

but I give her a slight grin
and muster, "I like your shirt."
I don't know how else to say it,

so I pay and leave for home.

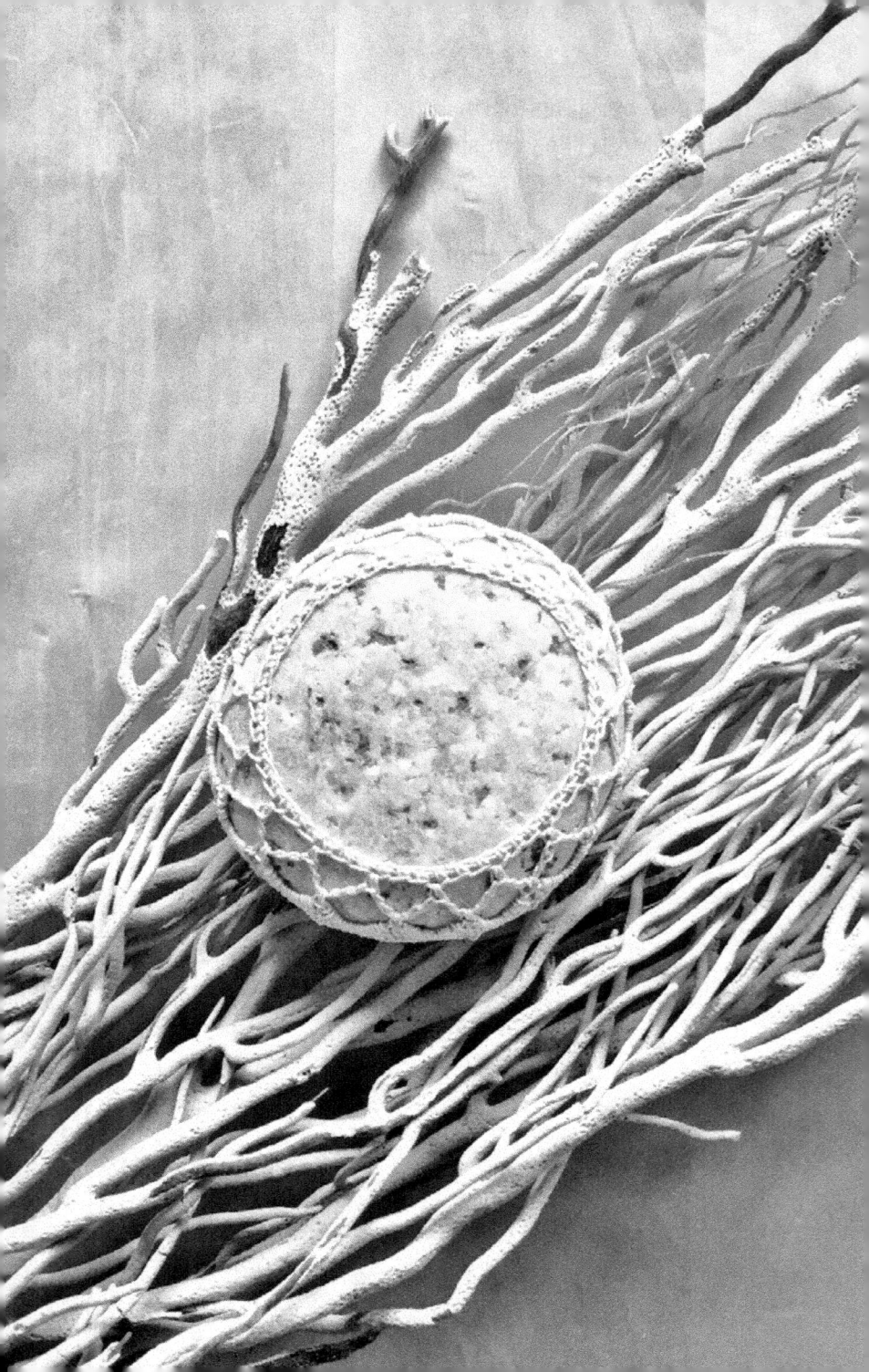

Acknowledgements

Previously Published

Thanks to these publications for publishing the following or previous versions of the following:

Al-Khemia Poetica, "I will not apologize"

Angel City Review, "Keansburg Park, 2012"

Black Napkin Press, "Circles for Words" "Slow Skinning"

Cadence Collective, "Black, the Consumption of Song" "Last Thread" "Passing Sounds Fade"

The Camel Saloon, "Pulp-Plastered"

Carnival Literary Magazine, "Good Friday Morning" "If Poetry Is Parked Car" "Sediment"

Cliterature Journal, "View at 4 A.M."

Cultural Weekly, "How to Go Backwards" "How to Unexist" "If you ask me what I want"

Drunk Monkeys Magazine, "Monkey Bars & Golden Spokes"

East Jasmine Review, "Scent Stained" "Unknown Employee"

Ekphrastic California, "Dead Song" "Unnamed Color" "When I've said all the words I can say"

Element(ary) My Dear Anthology, "Love Letter No. 4: To the Nail Biter" "Oceans Once Receded"

The Four Seasons Anthology, "What I Mean When I Say *Ageless*"

Heartbreak: Fuse Anthology, "Liquid Forget"

Hobo Camp Review, "Unanswered"

Incandescent Mind: Selfish Work, "To myself in grief state"

Indiana Voice Journal, "Girl in Flight" "Love Letter No. 3: To My Mending Self" "What I Mean When I Say Run"

In-Flight Literary Magazine, "Paper Airplane"

On the Grid Zine, "How I Stopped Naming Lost Things"

Poet's Haven, "Death by Rust" "Record Scratch"

Rainbow Journal, "Frost"

San Gabriel Valley Quarterly, "Reef of Clouds"

Shattered Anthology, "Conversations We Never Had"

Silver Birch Self-Portrait Anthology, "Love Letter No. 1: To My Pit-Bull Self"

Snorted the Moon and Doused the Sun: An Addiction Anthology, "Somatic" "What to do with empty hands" "Your Dark Sunlight"

Spectrum: An Anthology of Southern California Poets, "How Quiet Kills"

Spectrum 3: LoveLoveLove Anthology, "Diamond"

Spectrum 7: What's Your Heaven?, "Comfort of Cars at Night"

Tranquility Anthology, "Love Letter No. 5: To My Unsteady Breath"

velvet-tail, "Elephant" "Funeral for Bees"

Whiskey Fish Review, "What I Mean When I Say *We Can Talk Without Poetry*"

work to a calm: a confessional poetry zine, "Crescendo or What I choose to remember" "Damsel" "To the Men Who Told Me My Love Was Not Enough"

About the Author

Photo by Alexis Rhone Fancher

Sarah Thursday has been writing poems since she was a young teen. In addition to writing poetry, she designs and publishes books, hosts readings, workshops, and a poetry book club, as well as being a passionate advocate of poetry and the arts in Long Beach, CA. She was the co-host of 2nd Mondays Poetry Party and ran a poetry website called CadenceCollective.net. She has been published in many fine journals and anthologies and received a 2017 Best of the Net nomination for "To the Men Who Told Me My Love Was Not Enough." She has eight chapbooks, two poetry CDs, and another full-length book called *All the Tiny Anchors*. Many of her books are available at SadieGirlPress.com. Find and follow her to learn more on SarahThursday.com or Facebook and Instagram @SarahThursdayPoet.

Many thanks to the Long Beach poetry community and beyond, especially to those who are able to give support by showing up, virtually or physically. Huge thanks to the artist, Jennifer Takahashi, for her generosity.

About the Artist

Jennifer Tara Takahashi grew up near the ocean, camping across California and dreaming under chirimoya trees in her grandmother's wild back yard. This connection with nature is an important part of who she is as a teacher, artist and woman. She is an artist without the ability to commit to one material, since she enjoys the thrill of learning new techniques. Jennifer explores mixed media, watercolor, fiber arts, silk painting as well as creating crochet ocean meditation stones, fine silver jewelry and once-was-a-sweater plush animals. She creates art to convey serenity, love and to remind others of the joy and healing that connecting with nature can bring. With this in mind, Jennifer opened The Grateful Dandelion Atelier, a children's studio in Pacific Beach, California, which offers classes in yoga, mindfulness, storytelling and the arts. She looks forward to sharing the hand work, creativity and relaxation that her aunts, mother and grandmother passed on to her when they taught her the many crafts she enjoys. When she is not creating, you might find Jennifer dancing, reading, drinking tea, traveling or relaxing in the beach in Baja.